Tony,

Be Blessed!

May God continue to use you and grant you FAVOR!

10/2/09

Words of Essence

Publishing

Published by Words of Essence Publishing

© 2004 by LaWanda Lee

All rights reserved. No part of this book may be photocopied, reproduced, stored in or introduced into a retrieval system, broadcast or transmitted in any form or by any means without the expressed written consent of the Publisher of this book.

Library of Congress Card Catalogue Number: to be assigned
ISBN 0-976133-9-4 (trade paper)

First Edition
Second Printing, September 2005
10 9 8 7 6 5 4 3 2

Published and printed in the United States of America

www.WordsofEssence.com

Words of Essence

Acknowledgements

I want to thank you, Jesus, for birthing the vision and bringing it into fruition, in order to impact the lives of so many people.

Thanks to my parents, Larry & Wanda Lee and my brothers, Larron, Ladonte and Laurence for their encouragement and support throughout my life.

To Mary Satterwhite & Dr. India Reid for believing in me.

To Sadorian Publications and the staff and faculty at Durham Technical Community College for their much needed support behind the scenes.

Special thanks to the two ministries that are close to my heart:
Bishop Robinson and NC Miracle Revival Center Church and
Pastor Wooden, Youth Pastor Williams, and Upper Room Church of God in Christ for their spiritual guidance and for helping me to stir up the gifts within.

To my girlfriends, Chalice, Toni and Kisha for encouraging me to walk by faith and not by sight.

To Hubie Elliot, Leonard Sanders and Jermaine Johnson for pushing me to a level of excellence.

To all of my beautiful family members for your inspiration and love.

To others who supported me through prayer, encouragement and monetary blessings, Thank you!

Table of Contents

Empowerment
Part 1

A Word from The Lord . . 14
Endure 17
Free 18
Destiny 19
Persevere 20
Victorious 23

The Heart of Ruth
Part 2

You're Beautiful to Me . . 26
Metamorphosis 29
Thank You For 30
A Real Lady 32
A Real Man 34
Lonely, But Not Alone . . 37

Searching for Love
Part 3

Love is Like 42
Insecurities 44
An Illusion of Love 47
Thinking of You 50
Why I Can't Let Go 53

Realness & Truth
Part 4

Sorry Lord, 2004 60
Come Out the Closet . . . 63
Judgement Day 66
Chains 70
Question 73
Death to Life 76
Memories 77

A Glance into my Life
Part 5

Another Year More 80
My Annual Resolution . . . 83
Purpose 84
New Beginnings 86
Whispers 91
Why Wait 97

A Special Tribute
Part 6

A Virtuous Mother 102
Dear Dad 106
Preacher Man 108
A Shepherd's Heart 110

About the Author 112

All scriptural references taken from King James edition of the Holy Bible

Empowerment

Part 1

Ephesians 6:10

"Finally, my brethren, be strong in the Lord and in the power of His might."

A Word from The Lord

My child,
I see, hear and am aware
Of your many concerns.
My hand is not shortened,
Nor my ear heavy that my
Deliverance and salvation is unable to come.

For I am the Prince of Peace
And I offer peace to those whose
Minds are stayed on me.
I will dispatch my host of angels
To protect you from unseen dangers
And keep you in tranquility.

I am the Good Shepherd
You don't have to want for anything.
My rod and my staff they comfort you
Through the valley of the shadow of death
Evoking you to cast fear aside,
While opening your mouth to rejoice and sing.

Your sacrifice of praise moves me
And your sincere worship captivates my attention.
Do you honestly think that I would leave you stranded
In your abyss of troubles and confusion
Without sending you some form of intervention?

No, my child I love you too much.
Rest in me.
Wait patiently for me.
Don't fret because of evildoers
Or the plots and deviate traps that they construct.
For they shall soon be cut down like the grass
And wither as the green herb.
You shall look for them, but
They'll be no more.
For all who mess with my children
Shall be kicked to the curve.

In case you've forgotten,
Allow me to remind you just who I am.
I'm the King of kings, Lord of lords,
Creator of all and
The Precious Lamb.

Hurricane Ivan has nothing on me
For I control the winds and waters
And all of the inhabitants of the air, land and sea.

Instead of wanting to be like Mike,
You should want to be like me.
I'm holy, righteous, multi-talented, well-versed,
And the innovator of all skills and abilities.

What, the nations are still looking for Osama?
I know where he's at.
My presence is everywhere, at all times,
In the event that you haven't
Figured that out yet.

All of your impossibilities
Are simplities in my eyes.
I dry up cancerous cells,
Restore defected immune systems,
Break chemical and sexual addictions.
Any more problems?
Bring it on,
That too is a piece of pie.

I've come that you might have life
And have it more abundantly.
It's not my desire to see you struggling,
Dependent on the system
Or weeping hopelessly.

It hurts my heart
To see you weep and cry.
I'm full of compassion and
My mercies endure forever.
It was because of you that I died.

Imagine going through severe beatings and
Lashes to the degree that your flesh is completely distorted.
No friends, no peace, surrounded by haters and
Feeling like you've been aborted.

I know how you feel
Because my love is real.
I endured it all for your sake
To give you an expected end,
A means to salvation and
A place in the Book of Life for
Your name to be sealed.

So delight yourself in me
And I will give you the desires of your heart.
Your trial is only for a season.
It'll pass, your tears will be no more and
I'll give you a new start.

Please, heed my words
And bind them tightly around your neck.
I shall give you a prosperous end.
You haven't seen anything yet.

Endure

The Battle is becoming too intense.
I just don't see an ending to all
The pain and suffering.
Lord, this doesn't make any sense.
"My child, Endure."

Money is low and there's no food to be found.
All my bills are due at one time.
God I need your help.
No one else is around.
"My child, Endure."

But what about the lies and
Those who despise me?
What about the acts of jealousy and
Haters who attempt to kill me softly?
"My child, Endure."

"Remember that I will give you
Strength, peace and wisdom
To endure and overcome the complexities of life.
So don't be moved or easily shaken by
The appearance of Satan's knife.

No weapon formed against you will prevail.
You are an overcomer.
Everything will be alright.
Endure."

Free

Liberated and emancipated
From the
Cares of this life.

Unattached and uninhibited by sin and strife.

Unchained and unrestrained,
For depression and anxiety must release
It's hold.

Unshackled and unbound,
No longer carrying the heavy load.

I've been loosed!
I'm now Free!

I've been made a new being in God,
Redeemed by His blood,
As His Spirit abides within me.

He promised that He would never leave or forsake me,
But continue to abide by my side.
Oh yeah, I'm Free!

No more chains binding me.
Christ, the Liberator, has paid the price.
And for that reason
I choose to completely sell out to Him and give Him my life.

LaWanda Lee

Destiny

Are you
Walking, talking,
Seeing, believing and feeling
All that God has in store for you?

For He wants to take you through the doors,
That will take you
To the core of your dreams,
Your purpose,
Your
Destiny.

But it's all up to you.
So what are you going to do?
Because, nobody can hold you down;
No person, place or thing.
That's your dream.

And through
Christ,
Nothing is too extreme,
Although it may seem,
You know
What I mean?

So, keep walking,
Talking, living, seeing, believing
And feeling your
Destiny.

Through faith it will become your reality.

Persevere

Boisterous winds blew,
As the storm raged,
While Satan attempted to send various tactics
To take captive your soul
Like an innocent bird caged.

You were seeking God both night and day,
Ushering up prayers and praise
While
Researching the scriptures
To see what God had to say

About the trials and tribulations
That were intended to keep you down.
And sadly when you needed
A shoulder to lean on
No one could be found.

Money acting funny,
Issues with your job, family and friends,
People telling lies,
You would cry,
"Lord, when will this chaos ever end?"

But, I hear the Lord saying,
"I will provide you with guidance
Concerning what to do
And where to go.
I see you tithing and giving faithfully,
Remember, you'll reap what you sow."

Giving of your time
To minister to the kids,
Evangelizing to the lost souls about Jesus;
His life, death and resurrection,
And the miracles that he did.

Sharing your personal testimony

Of the life you went through
As evidence to others, especially young kids,
That this thing about
Christianity is true.

Many have been delivered,
Being touched by your love.
Without hesitation,
You see a need
And immediately pull out your check book,
Denying your pleasures
To push others above.

Above your personal wants,
Desires and goals.
Sometimes putting your interests on pause
And your plans on hold.

You embody the spirit of David,
Having a heart after God's own,
The leadership of Joshua,
As you recall that
God will never leave you alone.

He'll never put more on you than
What you can bear.
He said that He'll never leave or forsake you,
He'll always be there.

He said to count it all joy during
Those moments when
You're tested and tried.
Don't become weary in well doing,
Or easily moved by those
Who may have lied.

For there's coming a day when
God shall wipe all your tears away,
And you'll be raptured up to your heavenly home,
For eternity you'll stay.

Keep your head up
And continue to persevere,
Because you are a child of God.

Many blessings are coming your way.
So, get ready to enjoy the ride!

Victorious

The road was extremely rough and long,
But you made it!

The problem intensified and
Became even more complicated,
But you accomplished it.

The fear of failure enticed you to not even begin,
But you persevered and completed it.

Frustrations may have encouraged you to give up,
But you endured it.

The roller coaster of life led you through
Tunnels of uncertainties,
But you stuck with it.

Finally, distractions of all kinds aimed to
Get you off course,
But you conquered it.

Through the ability of Christ,
Combined with your
Patience and determination,
You successfully overcame your obstacles and
Gained the Victory.

Congratulations, you did it!

The Heart of Ruth

Part 2

Matthew 6:21

"For where your treasure is, there will your heart be also."

You're Beautiful to Me

Thus saith the Lord,
I love you for who you are,
Not for what you're trying to become.
I'm attracted to the pureness of your heart
Contrary to the thoughts of some.

With me it's not about money,
Materialistic possessions or popularity.
These things are all vanities reflecting
No essence of spirituality or stability.

I understand that Hollywood presents you
With a message that is just the opposite:
Multi-million dollar cribs,
Big butts and big breasts,
Little waist and little heels.
They're promoting a combination of walking
Barbie dolls and Eurocentric qualities
That are unreal.

No one's satisfied with my work,
Which is the reason for cosmetic surgeries,
Lip suctions, implants, reductions
And other alterations.

If these methods were legit then
Why so many dissatisfactions?
Eating disorders, depression,
Low-self esteem, self-isolations
And other issues perplex females
Daily even after their beauty operations.

Baby girl, you are beautiful to me.
I made every atom, cell,
Bone and muscular structure
That makes up your anatomy.

Before you were even thought of
I was thinking about you.

LaWanda Lee

Sure, I know that guy told you that
You are always on his mind,
But you know honestly that's not true.

The thoughts I have of you are
More than the particles of dry sand.
My thoughts involve giving you
Hope, a bright future
And an expected end.

I made you just the way you are;
Some big, some small,
Some short, some tall.

So why are you trying to mimic
Tyra Bank's show,
"Top Model?"
As I forementioned, those girls will never
Be satisfied until their void is filled
And they choose me to follow.

I want you to know that you
Are not a sex object
Or a pair of legs that parades
Before the eyes of men.
Your purpose is greater than
Feeding their visual appetites,
Or trying to obtain a certain size, height,
Or weight to appeal to vain measurements of
Becoming beautiful and thin.

You are fearfully and wonderfully made.
Marvelous are my works.
I formed your intricate parts and
Covered you in your mother's womb.
All flesh was structured
Creatively from the dirt.

So, shake off all insecurities
And walk with your head held high.
You are my bride to be

And the beauty of my eye.

Remember, you're beautiful to me!

Metamorphosis

Lord, how amazing you are!

Transform me.
Make me more like you.

Become the leg that I stand on,
The hand that I hold,
The voice that whispers a message from above
To uplift and encourage the soul.

When my mind becomes distracted by the cares of this life,
Shift it to the things that are
True, noble, just and right.

And if my eyes despise others with looks that are impure,
Help me to mimic
The look of compassion you gave to men,
While making yourself
The ultimate sacrificial cure.

When my feet seek to tramp on those that
I very much dislike,
Let me bless those who curse me,
Pray for those who use me,
And do good, despite.

When my mouth drives itself to gossip about
The short-coming of others,
Let me examine the mote in my own eye,
By encouraging and inspiring those around me,
Instead of taking part in the transferal of lies.

Transform me, Lord.
Make me more like you.
Only you are perfect and have the ability to make me new.

Thank You For

Thank you for the air I breathe
And for creating nature and
The beautiful flowers and trees.

Thank you for giving me eyes to see
Your wonderful creation
And ears to enjoy the vibrant sound of humans,
Exotic animals and oceanic motions;

The sound of waters clashing against the land.
It amazes me to think that you designed the earth
And all of its components
With a simple phrase,
"Let there be,"
Instead of needing multiple hands.

Thank you for the ability to use my
Tongue and teeth to taste treats like
Chocolate, cotton candy, caramel,
And indulge in a good ol' fashion
Soulful southern feast.

Thank you for giving me a nose to distinguish between
Grotesque and sensational smells.

Thank you for two hands
Comprised of eight fingers
And two thumbs,
Permitting me to feel the warmth of
The sun's rays beaming on my skin
And the frosty winter winds chilling my body into a state
Of becoming numb.

Thank you for a mind to think about
The future, present and past.
And the intellect
To make difficult decisions about
What, when, where, and for how long a thing will last.

LaWanda Lee

Thank you for giving me a heart to express
Eros, philious, and agape love.
And thank you for giving the ultimate sacrifice,
The gift of your only begotten Son.

Words can't describe or attempt to capture
The fullness of my gratitude,
It's true.

I appreciate you for making me
Who I am,
Forming my unique physical structure,
And giving me senses
To experience life
Through You.

A Real Lady

Diamonds, furs and lace are nice.
Chocolate, strawberries and fudge are delights.
Fancy dinners, cruises, and world tours
Are pleasant sights.
But a real lady is one who
Forsakes all and
Follows Christ.

The whispers of sweet nothings
Are all things of the past.
She doesn't rely on a man
To define or complete her.
The scriptures build her confidence
And give her
Determination to last.

She acknowledges the Lord first
Before she makes a step,
By seeking him early in the morning,
Praying, fasting,
And reading his Word for
Guidance, understanding and a deeper depth.

A real lady lives a life of virtue
And walks with an essence of grace.
She respects her body,
Protects her reputation
And guards her heart
As though it were a delicate vase.

She affirms her brothers
By convincing them
That they are awesome men of God.
She uplifts her sisters
With encouraging words,
While lending an attentive ear
For them to confide.
She's not to be approached with
Cheap cat calls

LaWanda Lee

And thuggish hand signals by
Kats with baggy pants showing their drawls.

You'll never find her at a sweaty club
Trying to get her freak on,
Or on the corner of 3rd Street wearing
Six inch heels with
A pair of low-rider jeans
Showing her thong.

No, a real lady occupies her time with
Issues that are close to God's heart.
She loves ministry.
She loves people.
She loves influencing others to give up
Destructive ways in exchange for a fresh start.

A real lady is patient.
A real lady is kind.
She works skillfully with her hands
And is productive with her time.

She resembles a rare ruby
Hidden in a treasure chest.
She's independent,
But yet,
Dependent on God,
Which distinguishes her from all the rest.

A real lady,
That's what she is indeed.
The man of God that seeks and finds her
Will be blessed
As they both allow
God to continue to
Guide, instruct and lead.

A Real Man

A Real Man,
Is that you?
Well, let me spit some knowledge
To see if it's true.

My brother, you were uniquely designed
In the image of God.
From the beginning,
Your distinct features,
Your three-fold being established you with
Preeminence and dominion
Over all the creatures,
While God left you tending the garden
To keep you occupied.

So, what is a real man?
He's one who completely follows God.
Contrary to what
Jerry Springer or Ricky Lake portray,
He's not thuggish, effeminate, lazy,
Neither does he treat women like Burger King;
Have it your own way, right a way.

A real man has a heart like David,
Is persistent like Paul,
Has courage like Joshua,
Shows compassion like Jesus to all.

A real man understands the importance
Of getting a prayer through.
When faced with
Uncertainties and complexities
He falls down to his knees on behalf of
Family, friends and even his enemies.

He confesses with his mouth and
Believes in his heart that Christ is real.
For he knows that the void in his soul,

Outside substances, people, places or things,
Can't begin to fill.

He doesn't conform to the world's
Philosophies or the latest fads;
Creating pseudo images,
Wearing tons of ice and
Building his hopes and dreams on
Grimy videos that won't last.

A real man doesn't give up
When he makes a mistake.
He realizes that
He can do all things through Christ
And that no one promised that
Life would be
A piece of cake.

A real man doesn't vent
His frustrations out on his girl
Or beat his wife like Ike.
He doesn't disrespect his mother or
Dis his father,
Although he may not have been
Present during the early stages of his life.

A real man is patient,
Yet persistent when it comes
To the things that he wants.
Once he takes it to the Lord and
It has been approved,
Then and only then does he make his move.

Especially, when it comes to
Looking for a mate,
Silly, easy, or loose beautiful chicks
Without Christ
Will not be selected as his date.

A real man should not be viewed by women
As merely a walking ATM
Or a six-pack coupled with
Biceps and triceps,
Rolling on a nice set of rims.

No, he deserves to be respected, honored
And seen for the man that he is.
He's not her sugar daddy
Or her pimp,
But is fearfully and wonderfully made,
Even down to his cells,
Muscular structure and limbs.

A real man,
Is that you?
Only you can answer that question
And decide if it's true.

Lonely, But Not Alone

God, I feel so lonely.
I feel like no one understands.
I feel so empty inside my soul.
I need a touch from your gentle hand.

For so long I've tried to satisfy that
Empty void in my heart with man's love;
Desiring attention, longing for his touch,
Hearing his soft words in my ear,
Any sign that would convey that
He loved me very much.

Someone who'll sweep me off my feet and
Take the pain away
Or wipe the tears from my eyes when
Life reverts into a gloomy day.

Hollywood makes life seem so simple.
It projects a blissful utopia comprised of
No cares or worries,
The perfect job, perfect house, and
Perfect children with dimples.

But that portrayal of reality is
Opposite of what's before me;
Racism, sexism, and
Discrimination of all kinds.
The love of many has waxed cold and
The devil has completely
Taken over people's minds.

God, I need some peace for my mind.
I need comfort for my soul.
I need reassurance that all is well
And that I won't be left alone in the cold.

I need you to tell me that you'll
Wipe away all the tears from my eyes.

I need you to show me that I won't continue
To be held in bondage falsely
Because of all the lies.

God I need you.
No one else will do.
You are my joy in the time of sorrow,
My comfort when I'm going through.

Unlike man,
You would never leave me
Stranded in a desert to die.
You would never turn your back
Or close your ears to my sincere cries.

You would never laugh or mock me
When I accidentally stumble and fall.
You would never cheat on me or hurt me
Or attempt to make me feel small.

God, you would never exploit my body
Or use me for a cheap thrill.
You would never manipulate my emotions
In order to seal a selfish deal.

You would never intentionally avoid me
Just because I did what I thought was right.
You would never just throw up a peace sign,
But for me you'll be willing to fight.

God, I know that you would be there for me
Through thick and thin.
I know that I can trust you with my life and
Give you my heart to mend.

I know that although I'm lonely,
I'm never alone,
For you are always there to whisper an
Encouraging word and
Give me strength to go on.

LaWanda Lee

Ol' soul, why are you cast down?
And why are you disquieted within me?
I must hope in God and
Continue to praise Him.
He'll never leave
Or forsake me.
He'll release
The chains of bondage
And make me free.

Searching for Love

Part 3

John 15:9

"As the father loved me, so have I loved you: continue ye in my love."

Love is Like

Love is like ice cream on a hot sweltering day.
Each drop cools down the driest parts of the body and
soul,
Allowing even the most sorrowful person
To smile and say

That life is worth living and my love is worth giving,
And although I can't change the errors of my past,
I'm working hard today to make sure that
My future will last.

Love is like giving all you can give until
You can't give anymore,
And then looking for nothing in return or
Ever closing your door.

Love is like saying a kind word even when it hurts so bad,
And smiling although that person has done everything in
Their power to make you mad.

Love is like placing the blinders over your eyes toward
Someone's weaknesses and faults,
And then placing magnifying glasses on to describe
Positive attributes not easily demonstrated or sought.

Love is like saying, "I'm sorry" even when
You're convinced you didn't do any wrong,
And then lending your shoulder in the time of need for that
Same person to lean on.

Love is like you, Lord.
I was the one who did you wrong.
You loved me despite my iniquities and the repetitive
Apologies followed by the same ol' sinful song.

Your love is patient.
Your love is kind.
It bears all, believes all, hopes all, endures all,

LaWanda Lee

Regardless of the penalty or the fine.

Even when my transgressions crucified you all over again,
You didn't knock me or kick me to the curve.
No, your grace was sufficient even then.

I'm so glad that I've experienced your divine love.
Please help me to reciprocate it back to you
And share it with others, who are also called,
"Your beloved."

I mean, if you can forgive and love an ex-sinner like me,
It should be easy to show compassion for others,
Especially my enemies.

So, ultimately love is like seeing the world
Through your eyes
And denying my personal wants and desires,
In order to exemplify the love you displayed when
You gave your life to die.

Thank you for showing me what love is like.
I think I'm ready to put it into action now and
Begin to make you my delight.

Insecurities

Vulnerabilities,
Instabilities,
Hear the cry of Insecurities.

I don't like my legs.
I don't like my hair.
Why do people always have to stare?

My nose is too big.
No, I think it's too small.
I wish that I could redesign my face,
Body and all.

My hips are too wide, but
In jeans they look flat.
I wish I were like the other girls
Who have more back.

Why does my hair have to be kinky?
I wish it were long and straight.
I need more bounce so that it can
Move with the wind
And shake.

My lips are too full.
I wish I could deflate
Them a little.
Maybe then I could look like the other models.
Yeah, that would be cool.

And my eyes are too dark.
I need them to be lighter.
Maybe hazel, light brown, a tint of green,
It doesn't matter.

There is so much more wrong with me.
I can't find much right.
But, maybe I should try to

LaWanda Lee

Think about others,
Instead of myself all day and night.

Like, what about the girls who don't have
Arms or legs,
They have eyes, but can't see
And ears, but can't hear.

They lack the ability to
Dance, sing, play or
Feel objects that are near.

They wish they could
Trade places with me and
Would definitely flaunt my body happily
And not even
Think about the flaws or
Deficiencies.

Matter of fact,
They wouldn't call my body
A mistake,
Because it was something that God created.
And on a scale from one to ten,
His works are
Perfectly rated.

God,
Forgive me for downing your creation.
I should be thankful for how
You made me,
Not envy others or
Wish for maybes.

I shouldn't let insecurities
Whisper into my ear,
Or vulnerabilities
Creep into my thoughts.
You said that
I'm precious, delicate and a jewel to be sought.

So, as I look into
The mirror,
It's a new creature
That I see.
I see intelligence,
Ambition,
Talent, and beauty.

Thank you Lord
For making
Me
Uniquely and creatively.

An Illusion of Love

I thought you were the one
To make my life complete.
I didn't consider my parents, close friends or others.
No, I pushed them away and fell in love with
Your mind, spirit, and of course, your physique.

I poured my heart out to you as you
Whispered sweet nothings into my ear,
Telling me how cute and fly I was;
Sweet, hot and chocolate like a delicious musketeer.

Day in and day out, I pondered about our unique love.
I didn't have my father in my life to tell me
That I was as beautiful as a dove.

So when you stepped on the scene exemplifying
Compassion, sensitivity and romance all in one,
I eagerly threw down my guards
And in my heart I allowed you to come.

You see, I longed to hear someone tell me
Those three simple words, "I love you."
And when it finally came from you, boyfriend,
Sista girl was through.

But, you didn't stop there with your intense lustful stares.
And I was so blinded by what the world defined
As love that I didn't even care.

I wasn't trying to hear the words of wisdom from my mom.
She said, "Baby girl you better put God first,
Because carrying a baby and genital warts,
Clearly is not the bomb."

But when the mood was right and
The lights became a little dim,
All I could think about was being close to him.

Seconds became minutes,
As minutes progressed into hours,
And I began to open up unto him like a blossoming flower.

We slept the night away.
Away, away, cause when daybreak came
The guy that I entrusted my heart and soul to didn't stay.

Alone again was what I became.
Feeling hurt, shame, and guilt
As my heart bled openly like the rain.

Oh God, this was not how things were supposed to be.
I thought that if I gave Him my body,
My love he would feel and see.

Oh man, was I so ever wrong.
But, I guess it's too late now.
So, I'll just make myself available and to
The other guys, here I come.
But wait, my mom always said that your word is true.
And if that's legit then
Your love for me protrudes like the morning dew.

You said in your Word that I was
Blessed in the city and blessed in the fields
And everything that my hands touched,
Prosperity and divine favor would fill.

You told me that I must repent of my shortcomings
And all the other bad things I do
And present my body as a living sacrifice,
Which is my most reasonable service unto you.

And if your word is true, I know that my manifestations,
That is, those things that I see,
Are not indicative of my revelations,
Which are the awesome things that will soon be.

And for that reason, I know that you've already

Given me a clean start and
Are preparing for me a real man of God,
One who is close to your heart.

A man who will love me, like Christ first loved the Church.
And who will attend to my every need,
Even on down to my deepest hurts.

One who won't exploit my body for a few minutes of fun
And then echo my business up and down the streets
Of how the action was done.

Oh no, God's beautiful creature
Will walk in the fruits of the spirit at all times.
And he'll sing to me Songs of Solomon
Diced with love, passion and hot rhymes.

Most importantly, my man of
God will treat me like a queen,
A virtuous woman empowered by the Almighty
To do great and marvelous things.

So, you see boyfriend, I may have slipped up
Once, twice or maybe even more,
But God's love is perfected within me
And for that reason
I will seek Him faithfully and wait patiently
Until He unlocks the door.

My fantasy is God's reality.

And my illusion of love
Will transpire from the heavens above!

Thinking of You

Roses are red
And of course violets are blue,
But concerning my feelings for this particular guy
I'm not sure what is true.

It started as a mere friendship laced with
A few games of basketball,
But then there came fancy dinners, movies
And late night calls.

All of which drew
Me closer to him,
But most importantly his love for God
Was genuine and tighter than
Any 22 inch set of rims.

In everything he did
He would consult God.
If I needed any assistance of any kind
He would make an effort to provide.

The strange thing is that based on my track record
He's not the typical guy that I would
Be attracted to,
But some weird connection occurred
Pulling me close to him like glue,

Longing to be near him,
Hear his voice, see his smile,
Feel his touch or even endure the things
That irritate me while

I commence to saying that
I want to remain single and free.
I enjoy my freedom and the independency flare
Projected in the media by the new millennium woman
And the group Destiny.

LaWanda Lee

Although I don't endorse all of their ideologies,
I feel it's important to be assertive, confident, and not
Solely dependent on a man.
My mom always told me to travel, work on your career,
Obtain a second degree and get all you can.

In realizing that marriage is a lifetime commitment,
You don't want to go in feeling like he stopped you
From doing and becoming more.
So take advantage of your time and youth,
While allowing God to help you explore different doors.

She told me that it's important to
Bring something to the table.
A cute face and a smile with no skills
Will certainly destroy a relationship and marriage
And turn reality into a fable.

So with regards to this guy
I find that he's becoming the apple of my eye.
I don't want to like anyone.
I want to be free, but my heart says the opposite
No matter how hard I try.

Originally I thought that life was about
Chilling with my girls and having fun,
But since he's no longer in the picture,
I've realized what the impact of his presence has done.

From the crown of my head,
To the soles of my feet,
I've made alterations with his help
That have significantly made me more complete.

Spiritually he's challenged me to
Research God's Word,
While praying and seeking the face of God
Until I receive an answer from above.

So why is it that it's so difficult

Searching for Love

For me to commit?
Maybe it's just not my time or season.
Or perhaps, fear of the unknown
Creeps into my mind and sits.

True, it may not be my time and
I may have a little fear,
But there are a few things that disturb me,
Creating hesitancy to draw near.

Sometimes I feel that he
Doesn't believe or trust the things that I say.
Or maybe that previous girlfriends
Have skewed his perception of females
Causing him to be overly protective,
Feeling that she may cheat,
Hurt or use him for his money.

And then again my theory may be completely false.
It might just be God's will for us to remain genuine friends,
Leaving the past in the past
And counting our friendship as a gain,
Instead of a loss.

I will submit that our friendship is special and unique
It is comprised of spiritual encouragement,
Advancing for the better,
And pressing toward the mark is what we
Implore each other to seek.

Concerning this particular guy,
He is certainly one of a kind.
He'll always hold a special place in my heart
As a brother, a friend, and
Awesome man of God.

LaWanda Lee

Why I Can't Let Go

I think about you all the time.
You circulate like hands on a watch,
An ellipse in my mind.
I know that I should let you go,
But it's so hard, and if I miss a beat
It might disrupt my entire flow.

You tell me that you love me
And that I'm the one for you.
The one who understands, cares and feels you,
Who even interprets your thoughts
When you're going through.

I wish I could just walk away
And let things be.
You know, detour my focus onto
Work, family, friends, and church,
All the beautiful components that make up me.

But for some reason, I feel there's a piece missing
From that puzzle that I call life.
And strangely, I've convinced myself that it's you.
Your love pierces me like a double-edged knife.

Many guys have come my way
Kicking lines that I'm cute and sweet,
Extending the offer to become their girl,
Eventually their wife,
And have a few kids to make our lives complete.

But for some reason, I can't open up,
Or even give them a chance.
An opportunity to explore my heart,
Share my thoughts,
Or give them my last dance.

God, I'm so perplexed and
I don't know what to do.

I know that you prophesied through many
That you were preparing for me a husband,
One with a heart of God, who'll love me for me,
And be true to you.

But, my question still yet remains,
"Is this guy the one for me
Or am I wasting my breathe and energy
On someone who can never be?"

I know you said in your Word that
Good things come to those who wait.
And that you would give me the desires of my heart
Regarding every aspect of my life, including my mate.

I mean, I'm not trying to move too fast
Or get out of your will.
But, it seems like this guy on my ranking scale
Is not just a dime, but a hundred dollar bill.
He seems to possess all of the qualities
That I desire in a mate,
To the extent that I'm willing to see him
On a level beyond just an ordinary date.

So why do I feel so strongly about this guy
To the point of omitting others from the picture
And positioning him
As the focal point of my eye?

And why can't I return to the way things used to be,
Move on with my life and let him go?
You would suggest that my weak flesh is screaming, "Yes,"
While my spirit cautions, "No."

I know that anything I put before
Or in the place of you will be cursed with a curse.
And already situations are occurring between us
As if to hint that this relationship will not work.

So again, why can't I just take heed to your signs,
And deposit these feelings into the waste?
Or even stop pondering about him throughout the day,

At church or on my lunch breaks?

God if I must think retrospectively and
Be honest with myself
He was present emotionally for me
During a period of my life when my father wasn't there.
Soothing my fears, comforting me from worries,
And showing me that he cared.

As time progressed, I slowly substituted
Our sacred moments of quiet time and prayer
With late night calls and visitations,
Longing to peer into his chocolate brown eyes
With a gentle stare.

Leaving you like the 3rd wheel on a date
With no TLC, no moment's notice, like the movie,
"A Thin Line between Love and Hate."

Lord, I'm just trying to be real.
That's all I know to be.
I know that you want to be my Father, Lover and Protector,
The One that I call on first to help me.

Lord, in no way could I ever
Forget about you.
You've been my broad shoulders to lean on
During those moments when I was going through.

My love for you is first and foremost.
It is in and through you that I boast.
I know that you love me
With a godly jealousy.
And you will not permit unseen harm
Or danger to come me.

I also know that your sweet love
Is oh, so pure and genuine.
It doesn't ignite confusion or jealousy,
So what was really going on in my mind?

Searching for Love

Just the other day
I thought I had met the right guy.
I thought I had fallen in love
And could kiss my loneliness goodbye.

But God allowed me to see his true side.
And despite the fronting and camouflaged images
I've learned that when it
Comes to reality one can't hide.

Don't get me wrong,
In no way am I trying to project him as being bad.
I, too, have flaws, insecurities, blemishes,
And enough problems to make one mad.

But I did learn that no one can complete that
Missing piece to the puzzle that I call life.
That's Jehovah's job and if anybody or thing
Attempts to fulfill that role,
They will feel the edge of His knife.

Because God desires for me
To protect the anointing within,
To walk in ministry, remain a virtuous woman,
And cut away all weights of sin.

So, now I know the answer to my question,
"Is this guy the right one for me?"
The answer is, "No, he's not the one."
My true Rib, my soul mate to be,
In due season,
I will see.

Realness & Truth

Part 4

John 14:6

"I am the way, the truth and the life: no man cometh unto the father, but by me."

Sorry Lord, 2004

Dear God,
Sorry for the many times
That I let you down.
Instead of abiding by all of your commandments
I would follow my own agenda,
Leaving you with a frown.

Constantly putting you at the
Bottom of my list.
Or perhaps moving you to the top when convenient,
Treating you like a genie in a bottle,
Using you only to make a wish.

I wish I may,
I wish I might
Find peace, joy, and happiness,
Oh yeah, a new car, a fancy home, and a fine man,
Kind of like Sister "Right."

But God, these types of prayers
Fall deaf to your ears.
You're looking for a pure heart and clean hands,
Someone who with their entire spirit,
Body and soul will draw near.

A man or woman who will completely
Forfeit and surrender all
And come boldly before the throne
Releasing prayer, praise and worship like the converted
Brother Paul.

If American Idol, Ruben Studdard can issue
His sorry's for 2004,
But still keep going in and out of a revolving door,
I think that we should be real
And make our repentance list unto the Lord.
After all, it's He,
Not man, who holds
The keys to death and hell

LaWanda Lee

And is entitled to give us eternal rewards.

So allow me to begin.
Sorry Lord, for the time that
I compromised when my job
Required me to follow a dishonest request.
Instead of refusing to cater to their demands,
I went along with the flow,
Didn't want to cause any trouble,
I thought maintaining the peace was for the best.

But, you're calling for true soldiers who will uphold
The standard regardless of the cost.
Those who count their
Accomplishments and accolades as dung
In exchange for Christ,
Believing wholeheartedly that there's no loss.

Sorry Lord, for holding bitterness in my heart
Toward those who intentionally did me wrong,
Or for giving up the fight too easily,
Settling for second best
Or feeling like I didn't belong.

Sorry Lord, for doubting your word when
I couldn't see clearly
And allowing worry to become my best friend.
You said not to operate in fear, but to walk by faith
And my supplication you would send.

Sorry for the times I allowed my eyes to roam freely
In search of forbidden pleasures,
"Oh girl, look at him,
He is so fine
And his body is tighter than ever."

Let's keep it real!
You know how we do.
Lust and fornication are the major vices
That Satan uses to lure us to the end of our rope
Until we're through.

Leaving us exposed to all kinds of sins:
Genital warts, baby momma drama, soul ties, AIDs,
Heart break, abortion, masturbation, herpes, pornography,
Pregnancy,
The list goes on and on,
While the chaos only begins,

But God, when will this
Vicious cycle end?
The answer,
Only when we with a sincere heart
Recite our personal list of sorry's unto the Lord
And reverse 180 degrees leaving behind our sins.

We have to be real with God and
Put our emotions to the side.
People are dying and going to Hell daily.
It's time for us to be the Light and the Salt of the Earth,
Lending our ears and hearts for others to confide.

Dear God, we say sorry to you for
The sins known and unknown.
We ask you to cleanse our hearts, purify our minds,
And give us a clean slate
So that we can go boldly before your throne.

Sorry Lord, 2004!

Come Out the Closet

We ain't scared!
We ain't scared!
Or is this just another cliché?
The question remains,
Are we truly sold out for Christ,
To do his will, fulfill his will, and
Become true soldiers on the battle field
Each and every day?

Often times we preach and
Teach only within the four corners
Of our sacred walls,
Convincing each other,
Christians that is,
That Christ is Lord, a Healer, a Deliver and
The Savior of all.

But what about those who never
Enter the religious gates;
Plagued with false ideologies and
Post-modernistic views,
Feeling like they control their own lives
And God is simply fake?

Or have we considered the neighbors
Across the street,
Co-workers and buddies that we chill with
In the restaurants to eat,
Strangers and bystanders along the road
That we meet,
People in the mall, at the grocery store or
At the beach?

What about these?
They have souls.
Are they the exception?
Is that the reason why they have not been told?

God needs us to come out of the closet and
Feel his people, consul his people and
Share his love.
Someone took time out of their busy
Schedule to tell us how
Jesus died and paid the ultimate price for our
Sins and ascended to the heavens above.

Often times
"Give me, help me, bless me"
Are the prayers offered up day and night,
As we recline in our love seats,
Chilling, watching cable in our fancy cribs,
And taking it light.

But what about those who are stressed,
Depressed, possessed and
Dependent on pharmaceutical
Extractions to alleviate the pain.
Their gods are Brandy, Heineken, Marlboro,
Sex and cocaine.

Bound spiritually, mentally, and physically by
The chains of the enemy,
They long to be free, but cannot see that
Christ is real and powerful,
Because of the few vessels that are marred by
Sins and iniquities.

Confessing and professing Christianity in the
Eye sight of fellow saints,
Only to remove the mask,
Revealing their true selves:
Stealing, sipping on a lil' gin, sexing it up and
Other types of sins.

Too scared to go into the highway and bi-way
And leave their comfort zones.
Preferring to stay within the
Safe haven of the church.
No time to mess with the drunkards or

The homeless,
No, they choose to leave those Kats alone.

But it's time out for that closet religion
And that four corner wall salvation.
It's time to get bout it for Christ and expose
The devil's plans,
While demanding he loose God's creation.

It's time to start living the life that we profess
And begin to imitate God's love to the rest,
Especially those trapped in a mess.

It's time to stop saying,
"We don't have time,"
When in fact,
The Creator of time is imploring
Us to make a move.
Simply lay aside all agendas
And personal motives
And make Christ the center of our groove.

Attention!
Calling all Christians!
Going once, going twice…
"Come out the Closet!"

Judgement Day

What will you say?
What will you say on Judgment Day?

When your last report card
Has been announced,
Will it reflect S for Satisfaction
Or N for Needs Improvement,
Signifying that it's now
Time for you to bounce?

Oh, all the free time that you
Thought you had on your hands.
All the adventures and pleasures,
This was not the way you predicted
It would end.

Tick, tock went the clock of time,
Winding down slowly,
Now quickly, faster than ever,
As life flashed before your eyes.

This must be a joke.
It can't be real.
I'm only having a bad dream.
It must have been that spaghetti meal.

I'll wake up to my normal self.
I'm much too young to die.
Death is suppose to knock on
My neighbor's door,
I didn't even have enough time to say goodbye.

Oh no, it really is true.
I'm no longer living.
My life is through.

Lord, at least let me pray real fast.
Give me a second chance.

LaWanda Lee

I've always been a good person.
I didn't even go to that last dance.

And what about the many
Sunday services that I sat through.
Not to mention the bible studies,
Choir and dance practices, or
The Helping Hand Missions
That I used to do.

Lord, I know you have an excellent memory,
So, you should have all this down.
I helped that guy living on the streets
When no one else was around.

Then there was that time that
The Spirit was on me really strong,
I prayed for two elderly people and a lil' kid.
By the time I finished praying
They couldn't find anything wrong.

Oh yeah, I remember I used to talk to
So many kids about doing the right thing.
I helped them stay out of trouble and
Convinced them that it wasn't all about the
Nice cars or the Bling, Bling.

I think that deserves some recognition,
Considering it could have been the other way.
If it weren't for me,
Those kids would still be dealing and
Using drugs today.

So, Lord this is no time to be trippin.
You know, as well as, I know
That heaven is where
I'm supposed to be living.

My Boyz and Sistas are chillin
In their mansions on high.

Lord, you have to give me a break.
You must let me by.

But when all was said He shook His head and
Pointed to the Book of Life.
"Good works and noble deeds are nice,
But you never allowed Christ to
Deliver you from your sin and strife
And your name is not in my Book of Life."

But I thought that I was already walking
Down that narrow path.
And I had planned to shake the
Pastor's hand later on.
I had to get some things in order first
Because I heard that you were a
God of Judgment and Wrath.

God, please give me a second chance.
I'll do better next time.
I promise.
You should have told me these
Things in advance.

My child, many
Opportunities passed you by,
But you never gave me the time or day.
You would always say,
"Tomorrow, I will.
I'm not quite ready to give up my old ways."

Well, tomorrow has come
And your time is gone.
When I rang your number,
You never answered your phone.

So now I must disconnect.
I have another soul on the line.
Depart from me,
I know you not.

LaWanda Lee

Hell will be your home this time.

There are no parties
Or late night bashes.
No peace in sight.
Only torment and lashes.

So, for those who still have the chance
To answer the call from Christ,
Pick up the cell and don't delay
Tomorrow may be your today,

Judgment day is coming!

Chains

The chains of life have bound me
And my mistakes
Have led me to
A path of destruction.

The devil wants to see me drown in misery
Without the ability
To swim or function.

On one hand,
I see a beautiful light.
On the other,
A grotesque, dark night.

But if I've been bound
In chains this long,
Can change possibly be in sight?

Satan's convinced me that
It's all too late.
I blindly fell into his deviant trap
And bit into
His deceptive bait.

The bait which consisted of
Lies, pride, and
The pleasures of life.

It caused my eyes to open
Like Adam and Eve
In the garden when they hid with fright.

Sin camouflages itself as innocent gratification,
But once the tongue has tasted of its delight,
Its claws drag you helplessly
In a reversed direction.

All control and independency is lost

When Satan and sin become your Boss.

He comes in the form of
Additions, strongholds, and
Generational curses,
Which are lies.

He disguises himself in
The form of dysfunctional homes,
Disorders of all kinds and
Plants thoughts of
Self-hate and suicide.

He desires to steal, kill, and
Destroy your soul
And lead you into an abyss
Called hell for an eternal hold.

His plan is to make you
Doubt God's existence
And think that
Long life will always be.

After all, he's aware of his short time span
And is busy trying to convert many into
Satan worshippers
Instead of Christ followers,
Can't you see?

But the choice is yours and
Those chains can be released.
But, you must give your whole heart to Jesus
And resist Satan's tempting feast.

Realize that all pleasures last only for
A brief moment.
Is the satisfaction really worth
Months and years of consequences
That could ultimately lead to an eternity of
Fire and brimstone,

Where the worms are never dormant?

Your soul is too precious
To let it go to waste.

Remove the chains today
And receive freedom,
Life and
A chance to meet
Christ
Face to face.

Question

No one said that the
Road would be smooth.
That you would be liked by all,
Placed on a pedestal,
With all your needs met,
Never having to make a move.

The American dream consists of
Fame, fortune, and a life void of strife,
But then reality confronts us and unveils the
Struggles, complexities and disappointments
That plague this life.

It is this wretched world of sin
That attempts to oppress our souls;
Leaching onto our mentalities as if to attest
That You and I
Will never possess the ability to grab hold.

But grab hold onto what?
Well, onto the many blessings
And promises that God has in store.

If only we will hold fast to Dr. King's dream
By taking advantage of every opportunity
And constantly demanding more.

More respect, more freedoms, more liberties and
Of course, more services for our poor.
For, many of our ancestors were beaten and scarred
In order for the next generation to soar.

Their feet swelled intensively,
Pebbled with blisters and sores,
As they marched through the cotton and
Tobacco fields all day, every day,
While their masters sat and watched from the door.

But yet, we can't even get up and walk to the
School bus which is merely two minutes away.
Complaining that we're tired and sleepy,
And clearly, we haven't done a thing all day.

But we've forgotten that where we are
Has not always been,
And that innocent men and women were
Persecuted, placed in jail and killed
Although, they committed no sin.

We passively grip the back seats of the classroom,
Refusing to go to the front.
We waste our parent's hard earned money
Majoring to become a class clown
And specializing in performing silly stunts.

Within the black community,
Drugs and violence have become common place.
Fatherless homes, babies having babies
And STD's plague our race.

This is not what our ancestors envisioned,
But that we would walk with pride and
Integrity and make insightful decisions.

We must uplift each other and
Perform the best at everything we do.
We must write the vision and
Apply our hearts diligently until
Our dreams become true.

No longer can we settle
For second best and continue to make
C's, D's, E's and F's on our academic tests.

No longer can we continue to perpetuate the
Stereotypical images displayed on the screen.
You know, the thug, the ho, the playa and
The hypocrite who acts holy only to be seen.

LaWanda Lee

No, those days are gone and through.
It's time for us to convert our speech
Into action and begin to just do.

For, no one said that the
Road would be smooth.
That you would be liked by all,
Placed on a pedestal,
With all your needs met,
Never having to make a move.

Sure, the American dream should consist of
Fame, fortune, and a life void of strife,
But reality shows us that we must
Take advantage of every opportunity and
Do something with this life.

Question…
What are you going to do?

Death to Life

Wipe your eyes.
Please don't weep.
Know that your loved one is only a sleep.

Resting briefly,
Only to open their eyes
To a better place on the other side.

A place of joy.
A place of tranquility.
A place of comfort,
Where there's no need for tight security.

No more terrorist attacks or fear of amtracks.

No more Tsunami swallowing up
Thousands of innocent lives.
No more hurricanes, earthquakes or mudslides causing
People to run and hide.

No more worrying about living from check to check,
Rent due, food is few,
Oh God, what am I going to do?

No more anxieties or catastrophes.

But when life here comes to a pause,
A new life will begin in heaven with the
Trinity and the angels.

From death to
Life,
Exist novelty in all.

Memories

Moments come
And moments go,
But what the future holds,
No earthly being
Can ever know.

We can only capture
The image of
Family and friends at that present time,
And then refer to them
As the years pass
In reflection of the good old days
That we left behind.

Precious moments
Are not only
A reflection of the past,
They embrace and foster the
Memories
Of life and emotions,
Allowing history a storage place
So that
As the years slowly crawl by,
Our memories
Will continue to last.

A Glance into my Life

Part 5

I Peter 2:9

*"But ye are a chosen generation, a royal priesthood,
an holy nation, a peculiar people,
that ye should shew forth
the praises of him who hath called you
out of darkness into
his marvellous light."*

Another Year More

Twenty-three years
You've blessed me to see.
Why you granted yet another year
Is completely oblivious to me.

Just the other day
I was learning to read and write,
Discovering mathematics,
Playing musical instruments and multiple sports,
While learning how to type.

I recall as a kid having hardly any worries
In the world.
I knew that when I called on mommy and daddy
They would come to the rescue to their baby girl.

However, once confronted with
More complex issues
Down that rigorous road called life,
I found out, Lord that it was you that
Held my hand, comforted me and delivered me
From sin and strife.

The moment that I found you and
Explored your realness
I knew I couldn't go back.
You proved yourself so many times
And even protected me, as a matter of fact.

Like the time that I swallowed a ketchup bottle cap
When I was two or three years old.
My circulation was cut off and
My skin became discolored,
But you made death release its hold.

Then there was that 6th grader at the YMCA.
I was only in 3rd grade when behind
The double doors he attempted to rape me.

LaWanda Lee

"Please, please don't do this,"
Was the only thing I could say.

He had removed his swim trunks as
He tried to hold me down
And I knew it was your angel sent to the rescue
Because he peered into my eyes,
Released his grip and
Walked away never to be found.

Or what about my senior year in
High school when
I tore my ACL playing tackle
Powder puff football.
Not only did you bless me with a speedy
Recovery after surgery,
But also to be crowned "Maid of Honor"
On the Home-coming Court in front of all.

I recall in college my freshman year
Walking by myself
Around midnight after studying in
The library halls.
Twice, two homeless guys approached me by the
Arboretum demanding money.
When I looked around there was no one except
On you, Lord to call.

One guy looked above my head with fear
Wrapped inside of his eyes
And ran as though he had seen a ghost.
No one else was around,
So I knew it was you again,
For my security, you had sent your angelic host.
The second encounter could have really
Led to my end,
But you directed me to talk to him kindly,
Share your love, give him a couple of dollars,
After leading him into prayer about his sins.

Remarkably, I knew he had felt your touch.
For this same guy with tattered clothing,
Matted dreads and blood shot eyes
Was now crying, his eyes now white,
And calling on your name, like such.

And even presently with losing my job,
I know that it was all in your will.
Already you've granted me favor with
The publication company,
Blessed me with four new poems,
To witness at the unemployment office,
Make contacts with many, and form other deals.

This has been my most
Challenging obstacle yet,
But I'm sure if you've
Brought me this far in victory
This test will pass also and on the solid rock
My feet, you'll set.

God I can go and on about your
Many acts of love.
But one thing is for sure,
You've got this 23 year old lady
Wrapped tightly in your divine glove.

Despite the many times that
My destiny and purpose
Satan has tried to devour,
Every year you've shown new mercies
And have taken me higher.

LaWanda Lee

My Annual Resolution

To boldly walk through the
Doors of Opportunity
That I allowed to slip away
Due to fear.

To take out more time to experience the
Joys of Life
With those I hold as dear.

To challenge myself spiritually by
Calling those things
That are not,
Into being,

While committing to commit
Not just half,
But all of me
To the One who is All-seeing.

Purpose

I have a purpose.
That's why I don't curse.
I have a purpose,
Each and every one of us.

I have no time to wonder whether or not
Someone is feeling me.
Or if the guys think I'm cute, ugly
Or fly as can be.

Or whether the sistas are threatened by my presence
Due to their own insecurities,
Whether my hair is too short or too long,
My complexion too light or too dark,
I have to be who God made me.

I have no time to sweat the small stuff
Because my purpose is too Great.

God called me to speak to the nations,
Lay hands on the sick,
And reach the unreachable before it's too late.

So while others are gossiping about
"Who's wearing what" or
"Who likes who,"
I could care less,
I don't know about you.

Our mindsets reflect who we are.
If we have the mind of Christ,
We can reach the moon and the stars.

That's why my dreams are Large
And my visions are Big.
Please don't confuse my zeal and confidence
For being a selfish or conceited pig.

For I realize that it's not my ability,
But the strength of Christ

LaWanda Lee

That will take me to the top.

Cause I've got purpose.
I'm writing the vision.
And my success,
No man
Can stop.

New Beginnings

On July 27, 2004
I was released from my job.
Interestingly, I told my boss that God had showed me
In advance, given me a spirit of peace,
And there was no reason for me to sob.

I smiled eagerly as the words,
"You're dismissed" rolled off of his lips.
I felt this incredible load emerge from my body.
I was free at last.
No more crying in the bathroom as the tears slipped.

Slipping down my face as
I talked to God daily about my oppressors.
Oh how they couldn't stand my joy or my praise,
As they intentionally placed more stipulations on me
To keep my voice censored.

Performing the job of two or three people,
Working 10-12 hours per day,
My boss continued to send mass emails of complaints,
But would not provide me with consistent assistance,
A simple, "That's your job, get it done"
Was all he had to say.

Oh God, multiple times throughout the day
I would retreat to the bathroom to get on my knees,
Begging you to recoil the tension and pressure
And place my mind at ease.

I would lift my hands and recite the scriptures,
I would bind and rebuke the devil,
And give a victorious shout,
While holding onto the nearest fixture.

All those moments flashed through my mind,
While in the conference room with the CEO.
I told him that this was all God's will,
My work was finished and it was time for me to go.

LaWanda Lee

I thanked him for hiring me straight out of college
And for giving me a chance.
I told him that I gained valuable skills
That I'll use at my next destination,
And strangely his eyes became glossy
As I tilted my head to glance.

I assume he was moved by
My speech of faith.
He opened his mouth and began to
Flower me with words of grace.

He complimented me on my integrity
And excellent work ethic.
He told me that if I ever needed a recommendation
He'd be honored to provide it.

I shook his hand and walked out of the door
To tell my co-workers that I would
No longer be working with them anymore.

Many were angry and mad,
Bellowing profane words out of their mouths.
One said, "You were treated unfairly,
They didn't give you any help,
You had no choice, but to tumble down south."

Yeah it's true about all the
Persecutions that I went through,
But God knows what's best and He'll open more doors
And provide guidance concerning what to do.

I cleaned out my office
As I released praise with my voice,
Thank you, Lord for deliverance.
That was perfect timing considering
It was already 6 pm, with 13 tasks left in queue.
Man, that's enough to make anyone rejoice.

The Spirit led me to return to my computer to
Send out a corporate email.
In it was my last goodbye, how God predestined

This door to close, and the verse,
"I can do all things through Christ."
It was evident that I had not failed.

The more I think about the sequence of events
And how things all went down,
I honestly believe this was premeditated and
The extra work load was purposed to make me bound,

Frustrated and with Discontent
And perhaps, to the point that I would quit.
But, my strength comes from the Lord and
I refused to give up.
So termination was the best way for them to make me sit.

When I was first hired by the company,
I was giving no formal training.
And three weeks later my
Former manager left on vacation,
Leaving me high, dry and clueless to manage
The entire contracts and ordering departments.

After three months of partially learning my job,
He was moved to another department.
Again, left alone to find my way through the system,
Calling carrier reps and utilizing any available resources.
This was definitely not in my initial job description.

But, the Lord proved faithful as
He allowed me to rise to the top.
Within a 5 month period of time I received
4 bonuses and a $5,000 raise.
I knew my fast progression would suddenly
Come to a stop.

Around December, I was given a new manager
To oversee my work and attend to my needs.
Still I had no in-depth training, solely going with the
Flow and trying to maintain good deeds.

The work load intensified as the company added more

External partners to the one we already had.
I requested to receive some assistance,
For already I was working from 8:30am to 7pm,
Sometimes to 8:30pm,
Which was really bad.

No assistance was provided.
So I inquired about receiving a raise.
I found out later that was a huge mistake,
For heavy scrutiny and performance documentation
Occupied the remainder of my days.

From that point on, my inbox became filled with
Petty emails from my manager regarding mistakes.
I will admit that some were mine and others systematic,
But my justifications were disregarded and swept away
Like debris with a rake.

Dear God, didn't they see?
I needed someone to come and help me.
With handling two departments and serving three
Companies mistakes were bound to occur more frequently.

"I was a done deal" and
I knew my job would soon come to an end.
Only I didn't know how it would happen
Or much less when.

In the meantime, the Lord encouraged me to be faithful
And maintain a positive attitude.
After all, it's all about Jesus and being a witness
So that on the hearts of man, the Holy Spirit can move.
Well, on that Tuesday evening in the conference room
My prediction came to past.
I guess this means no more working
Extreme late nights under stress.
Again, I'm free at last.

Overall, this experience has taught me three lessons
That will aid me in my walk with Christ.

First of all, trust in the Lord.

Place no confidence in man,
Because one day he'll place you on cloud nine
And the next day
Nothing you do will suffice.

Secondly, rejoice in the Lord always,
Letting your moderation be known unto all men.
They're watching your every step,
Documenting and trying to find fault
In whatever they can,

Because Satan hates Christ
And his followers with a passion.
He would love for the world to catch you slipping up,
Stealing, Cursing, fussing, and lashing.

Finally, I learned that the effectual fervent prayer of a
Righteous man or woman avails much.
God sees and hears all.
He'll bring divine intervention for such.

So, God I thank you for bringing
Closure to this chapter in my life
And
For providing me with a new beginning,
Guiding my feet and
Giving me peace, in exchange
For my worry and strife.

Whispers

Someone's on my shoulder
Whispering in my ear,
Telling me to do things I know
Will hurt God's heart
And prohibit me from drawing near.

Someone's on my shoulder
Speaking so smooth and seductively,
Encouraging me to lay down my standards
And integrity to sooth those yearning passions
That are screaming intensively.

Thoughts race through my mind
And cascade down into
The inner core of my soul
As my discernment becomes blurred,
While the voice entices me to look
At his eyes and his lips.
Oh, what a beautiful sight to behold.

No, I must put my flesh under subjection
And keep my emotions under control.
This brother just appeared from no where.
He could be the devil in the disguise
Trying to destroy my soul.

But he said that he was saved,
Loved the Lord and had a
Passion for ministry.
That he had settled down his playa, playa mentality
And was now in search for his "wife to be."

He said, "I believe it's you
That I'm attracted to.
I would love to spend some quality time,
Cook a romantic dinner, and
Even pray with you."
Someone's on my shoulder
Whispering, "Girl, he must be the one.

Relax, don't be so uptight.
Even God wants you to have a little fun."

"Why not," I think to myself,
"It's been a long time.
After all, he's a Christian, he loves the Lord,
And he certainly looks fine."

Smiles, words and numbers are exchanged
Before I walk out the door,
Only to receive a call a couple days later,
An invitation to the movies and dinner,
With intents on seeing me more.

Someone's on my shoulder
Imploring me to make the move.
"You're young and
There's no need to be lonely,
Even ol' Stella got her groove."
"You know, you're right.
What could possibly happen
With just going out one night?"

One night becomes two,
And two, three more,
But my spirit senses that something's not right.
I honestly don't think with this brother
There'll be a number four.

For although his words seem quite
Refreshing and pleasant to the ear,
His actions and behavior are not so clear.

On date number three
He wheeled me around his car.
He said we were going to get something to eat,
But quickly detoured to a remote area
Surrounded by trees and stars.

"Where are we going?"
I demanded to know.
He said, "Just sit back, relax

And enjoy the show."

We came to a stop
In an area unknown.
Doors locked, lights out,
As he reclined his seat backwards and
Began looking at me like a juicy bone.

"We need to talk.
You've been on my mind.
I've been thinking about your sexy lips
And how they would feel on mine."

Oh God, what have
I gotten myself into?
I need your guidance and protection,
For I don't know what to do.

I honestly thought that we were
Going to get something to eat.
Not once did I think that
I would become his personal treat.

"Can I get a hug?"
He said with his cheetah-like grin.
His eyes roamed up and down my body
As he gently stroked my chin.

Fear gripped my heart
As I grasped for breath.
Flashes of rape crossed my mind
And even the possibility to death.

Oh God, I really need you now
For no one else is around.

I need your Holy Spirit to convict his heart
And bind these lustful spirits down.

"Can I get a hug?"
He reached for my shoulders as
I shyly pulled away.

A Glance into my Life

He caressed me in his arms
With very little words to say.

I felt his warm breath rolling down my neck
As I pondered what would happen next.
"Girl, relax I would never hurt you.
I just want to spend some quality time.
I'm not in it for the sex."

He later added, "You're so attractive.
I wish I could just kiss your cheek."
He bent down slowly and touched that area.
Next, my lips he purposed to seek.

I stared out the window,
As if to convey a sense of apathy.
Yet, he moved closer, tilted my head
And stared into my eyes craftily.

Before I realized it, his lips had
Attached themselves to mine.
I can't lie, they were soft and delicate,
Which didn't lessen the temptation
Because home-boy was so fine.

Someone's on my shoulder whispering,
"You know you want to do it."
Honestly, I don't.
I'm not that type of girl and
I'm not trying to go through with it.

For I know that the eyes of the Lord
Are omnipresent, beholding both
Good and bad.
And regardless of how good this guy looks,
I can't give up my body and
Make God's heart sad.

Not to mention, lowering my standards
For a few minutes of pleasure
Would ultimately discredit my witness
And disappoint many others that I treasure.

But still the voice whispers,
"One time won't hurt.
No one will know, he'll be gentle,
He won't expose your dirt."

But one time is one too many
When you think about the consequence:
A possibility of pregnancy,
Disease, ruining my reputation,
And forming soul-ties that
Are difficult to dispense.
There's just too much to loose
And very little to gain.
And contrary to what society says about
Me trying to keep myself,
I'm not insane.

I'm not trying to walk into Satan's trap of
"I keep on falling in and out of love,"
"Riding on an emotional roller coaster," or
"Inviting all the guys in the neighborhood
Into my back yard."

I'm not a playa.
I'm not a ho.
I'm not easy.
So this guy might as well just go.

Yet the voice on my shoulder whispers,
"You're making a huge mistake.
He'll probably go back and tell his boys
That you were scared to kiss,
You're lame, corny and fake."

You know what, he can say and think
Whatever he wants.
Please,
For free, I'm not giving up
The milk or the cheese.

My father said that
I'm the apple of His eye.
And he demonstrated that by sending
His Son on the cross to die.

So with those thoughts in mind
I kept my composure.
He laughed flirtatiously,
Acting as if everything was kosher.

I held my own refusing to give in.
I didn't want to kiss, hug
Or do anything that would lead to sin.

Disappointed and perplexed
That he didn't get any play,
He took me back to my place.
God, thank you for helping me to
Resist this brother,
Allowing me to
Stay in the Christian race.

The voice on my shoulder
I didn't hear any more.

But I know it'll only be a season
Before he comes back
To tempt me some more.

LaWanda Lee

Why Wait

Why wait?
Everybody's doing it.
I hear it feels great and it's not very complicated.

Why wait?
The media promotes it,
Our favorite actors and actresses perform it,
And our schools endorse it.

Why wait?
We constantly see it,
We hear it and it's to the point that we can
Visualize and feel it.

Why wait?
It seems like it is the key that unlocks the door to
Popularity, attention and so much more.

More than what meets the eye,
More than what is actually seen when
The curtains go down,
When the popular cliques disperse to say goodbye.

More than the camouflaged expressions of happiness,
The giggles and laughs covering the hurt and pain,
The deep, unspoken secrets of actions that were in vain.

More than the confidential visitations to
The abortion clinics,
Or adding just one more number to
The millions of independents
Who've contradicted an incurable disease,
Trying to please others and seize the moment even if
It brought them down on bending knees.

Please, it's time to slow down.
It's time to breathe in and
Breathe out.

Does it really deliver all the fame,
Pleasure and clout
That people talk about?

Or is it like a vapor that comes and goes,
A temporary gratification that soothes the soul?
Only when it's over
Does the truth begin to unfold.

Was it really worth it?

Why wait?

I heard that everybody's doing it.
I heard it felt great
And that it wasn't too complicated.

Well, not until I heard the Truth from a different source.
I think that I'll continue waiting.
I've come too far.
I don't want to get off course.

A Special Tribute

Part 6

Dedicated to four influential people in my life:

Wanda Lee, mother, "A Virtuous Mother"

Larry Lee, father, "Dear Dad"

Pastor Patrick L. Wooden, Sr., "Preacher Man"

Bishop Shirrell D. Robinson, "A Shepherd's Heart"

A Virtuous Mother

Who can find a virtuous woman,
For her price exceeds that of rubies?
Who can find a virtuous mother
Who will go above and
Beyond the call of duty?

For nine months you bore the pain.
Disfigured your coca-cola bottle shape,
Forfeited pleasures, personal desires
And routine games.

Only to bring life into this life,
A being in the image of God.
You counted that worth it all,
Despite the turbulence
And rugged bumps along the ride.

Rising early and retreating late,
You made sure that the house was in order
And that your
Children, the neighborhood kids
And your husband all ate.

When money was low,
No food to be found,
You took nothing and made it into something
Through faith, prayer and praise, no devil
Could keep you down.

Your presence always lightens up
The darkest room.
Your soft words of encouragement
Dispels and eliminates any
Thoughts of doom.
Many women, including myself,
Wonder how you are able to maintain.
You juggle so many hats with your career,
Education, church and family,
Without even going insane.

Growing up in your house
I always felt your love.
You were at every practice, game, piano recital,
And academic event,
Lifting me up in your motherly glove.

Cheering me on and telling me
Not to quit.
Even giving me a pat on the shoulder
During the times on the bench that I had to sit.

Frustrated and angry with much discontent,
You would whisper
"That's okay
You can do all things through Christ.
That's a promise that God sent."

You've been there for me for all of my first:
First word, first bike, first speech,
Oh yeah and
My first boyfriend.
You gave me a few pointers that
For a life time I will definitely keep.

Growing up I hated wearing dresses
And I hated wearing skirts.
Please, the thought of
Sitting uncomfortably with
My legs closed was merely a curse.

But, being the virtuous woman that you are
You didn't give up hope.
Through soft words, a gentle spirit
And self example,
I felt my character aligning with yours
As you slowly pulled me into
Womanhood with a rope.

You taught me grace and style
And fashion with modesty,

How to convey a spirit of excellence
And professionalism
In the midst of mediocrity.

You told me,
"Be careful of what you do and say
For your name will go farther
Than you'll ever go.
Even if I don't see, God sees all
And you will always reap what you sow."

In regards to relationships you told me
To seek God first.
"Never settle for second best or lower your
Standards for cheap thrills.
For in the end, you'll be
The one who suffers hurt."

When it came to work, you said,
"Perform even the smallest task at your best.
Don't be afraid to put in long hours.
That is how favor is achieved, which
Allows you to soar past the rest."

In the area of spirituality you taught me
To work on fostering my relationship
With the Lord.
"Read your word, fast and pray,
Live the life that you sing about
And show forth God's love."

I can say that you've been my big sister,
You've been my girlfriend,
You've been my role model and
Most importantly,
You'll be my mother until the end.

One with a willing heart
Who always sees a need.
You sacrifice much in order for others
To be relieved.

As Proverbs 31:30 indicates,
"Charm is deceitful and beauty is vain,
But a woman who fears the Lord shall be praised."

We honor you today for your
Virtue and grace.

You're beautiful, classy,
Intelligent and assertive.

You're considerate, humble,
Diligent, and a true servant.

You've blessed the world with your
50 years of running this human race.

So sit back, relax and
Enjoy your day.

Your friends and family have gathered to say,

"Wanda Lee,
Happy 50th Birthday!"

Dear Dad

When I look into the mirror it's a part of you that I see.
I see your eyes, nose, lips and other distinct
Features inherited from you
And given to me.

I know that growing up we weren't the closest.
But over the years I've witnessed your display of love and
I know that as your only baby girl,
I'm your focus.

Although you were not as emotional as
I thought a father should be,
I grew to understand that you truly cared for
Me and the rest of your family.

It was the small sacrifices that I failed to recognize.
Like getting up in the middle of the night
To give me medicine for my tummy ache,
Considering you only had a few hours left
To sleep before you had to rise.

I appreciate you and mom for giving me
Lunch money for school
And picking me up from my many practices, games and
Other events that I thought were cool.

Thank you for escorting me on the field
To receive "Maid of Honor" on the Homecoming Court.
When I think back,
It was good just to have a father still living, breathing,
Walking, talking and things of that sort.

I remember looking in the stands and
Seeing you at some of my games.
You always wore a floppy hat and carried your camera,
Capturing every piece of action that came.

Or what about the billion times that my car broke down.

LaWanda Lee

You always came to the rescue and used your
Mechanical skills to fix it so that
I could continue to get around.

I'm certainly grateful for your
Financial assistance during my 4 years at UNC.
You helped me purchase books, food, and
Other supplies so that I could focus on
My academic excellence and be all that I could be.

Thank you for your words of advice
And for the spankings I received growing up when
I wasn't nice.

Thank you for kicking guys out of my room,
Although I didn't understand.
That's one of the many reasons that
I'm still keeping myself for marriage and
For the moment when
My future husband places a ring on my hand.

The many times that I failed to say,
Thank you
I hope this poem demonstrates my love and gratitude.

Dad, I truly appreciate you!

Preacher Man

"God First."
This is far from being a cliché, it is your lifestyle.
From the pulpit to the convenient store
You convey to all that
It's all about Jesus and nothing more.

Preaching the word in and out of season,
Boldly fighting against all kinds of demons.

Immorality, adultery, and homosexuality have to go.
Neither these nor any other sinful lifestyles
Will be tolerated or accepted on the low.

Holiness is always right and that's the message
That you preach day and night.

You pose as a role model to both the young and old men.
Teaching them the ways of Christ, masculinity,
And how to treat females with respect
That's genuine.

For the single ladies,
You exemplify the qualities that we should
Look for in a man.
You've taught us the importance of
Working diligently in ministry,
Keeping our standards high, and
Drawing closer to God at every chance we can.

Although, you may be troubled on every side,
You're not distressed.
For you know that God is slowly turning the corner and
restoring all back to you,
Leaving men to call you blessed.

The Spirit of the Lord is truly upon you,
Because he has anointed you to
Preach the gospel to the poor.

LaWanda Lee

He's given you the authority to rebuke the enemy,
Release the chains of darkness,
Deliver the oppressed,
The sick and the confused
As they enter the door.

So, continue to preach the Word,
"Preacher man,"
God has even greater in store.
You've significantly impacted my life,
As well as, so many more.

A Shepherd's Heart

Sound wisdom and discretion,
A man of honor and fortitude.
A vessel which seeks to serve, while
Compelling others to continue to press on through.

Countless times you encouraged me and
Helped me to realize my strengths
By providing platforms at a very young age
To sing, perform skits and coordinate other events.

You allowed me to hold the microphone
In front of the congregation,
Even though I couldn't really sing.

But you purposed to build my confidence and
Equip me for the greater opportunities that
God would later bring.

When I expressed concerns about the rise of
Premarital sex, disease and pregnancy among the teens,
You and the saints supported and implored me to coordinate
Seminars and programs that could intervene.

You and First Lady taught me how to fast during our
Three day solemn assemblies held every year for the youth.
I learned how to cry out to God with a pure heart and
Submit myself to Him like Ruth.

During our two weeks of camp meeting,
First Lady drilled in us that
"Women walk with grace, while men walk with honor
And that it was essential to know Christ for ourselves
Instead of having to wonder."

I am so grateful for the precious investment
That was made into my life,
Especially for overseeing my soul with a
Shepherd's heart while
Urging me to hold on knowing that
Everything would eventually be alright.

LaWanda Lee

About the Author

Lawanda Lee is a graduate of University of North Carolina at Chapel Hill. She currently resides in the Research Triangle Park area. She's the daughter of Larry and Wanda Lee of Selma, North Carolina.

Her passions include: writing & performing poetry, singing, dancing, playing sports and witnessing to the residents inside of the prison. She also enjoys challenging teens to walk in excellence through her lifestyle and in presentations on sexual abstinence, college preparation, and leadership skills.

With regards to poetry, she began writing in 2003 and the Lord has granted her opportunities to perform and minister spoken word at various churches, the Miss Black Teen Pageant of Johnston County, the Orange County Prison, over the air live with WCLY 1550AM, WAUG 750AM and WSHA 88.9FM, Duke University, the University of North Carolina at Chapel Hill and UNC- Greensboro, as well as, other events outside of North Carolina.

Her greatest accomplishment consists of giving her life to Jesus Christ and allowing Him to use her to impact the lives of others.